T0198647

Trapped in My Mind

Rescue Me

L.P. MD.,

authorHOUSE®

AuthorHouse™
1663 Liberty Drive
Bloomington, IN 47403
www.authorhouse.com
Phone: 1 (800) 839-8640

Published by AuthorHouse 01/25/2018

ISBN: 978-1-5462-2491-4 (sc)
ISBN: 978-1-5462-2492-1 (hc)
ISBN: 978-1-5462-2493-8 (e)

Library of Congress Control Number: 2018900635

Print information available on the last page.

Any people depicted in stock imagery provided by Thinkstock are models, and such images are being used for illustrative purposes only. Certain stock imagery © Thinkstock.

This book is printed on acid-free paper.

Because of the dynamic nature of the Internet, any web addresses or links contained in this book may have changed since publication and may no longer be valid. The views expressed in this work are solely those of the author and do not necessarily reflect the views of the publisher, and the publisher hereby disclaims any responsibility for them.

To all who have found their way out of a mind that has shut down to protect them, who have found themselves, from the bottom of my heart.

Love, death, memories, holding thoughts
Without knowing,
Holding life with passion and tears
Without knowing.
Remembering the good and bad, love and hate
Without knowing.
No names, no past, just the present with fate
Without knowing.
Passing through life, with the unknowns,
No names, just with an uncertain tomorrow.
Feelings for everything and nothing.
Passion for everything and nothing.
Numbness and pain,
Passion and rain, doesn't matter.
Just breathe, laugh, cry, and look for a mountain and climb.

Closing eyes, now you don't see.
No names, no need. For what?
Nothing matters in the end.
Past, present, future—it's just about faith.
And everything is without knowing.
Reality? Not sure. Just live, love,
And in the end, you will see the top of the mountain.
Having thoughts without having them.
What you see at the end of your climb doesn't matter.

The only thing that counts is probably nothing or everything.
Don't want to know,
Don't want to talk, see, or hear;
Everything and nothing,
Destiny or not, doesn't matter.
The end is without knowing, because the unknown is better or just because you don't want to know.

INTRODUCTION

I decided to write this book for myself and for others who have experienced disturbing moments in their lives. I had the most unpredictable and painful episode that a human being can go through. I hope that by sharing this with you can teach us, can teach me how to make a difference in the way people interact with each other. I hope that it can help us learn how to love and be compassionate and caring. However, I think all that is gone now. What you are going to read is not a work of fiction or a love story. The story in *Trapped in My Mind* is as real as the sky.

It chronicles a very dramatic episode that recently happened to me. We need to open our eyes and listen to the illness that might by present and, if so, might hit us badly. If I can change how people see and judge and react to just one person who is experiencing what I went through, that will be good enough. I will have reached my goal. That is why I am sharing my own story, sharing my mind. The events I will share in *Trapped in My Mind* are true events that impacted many lives, mostly mine.

When you see someone, anyone, wandering while talking to him or herself, what do you think? What comes to your mind? Probably nothing. Perhaps you just stared at the person. Or maybe you made fun of or simply ignored the situation. When it comes down to it, it's a question that most of us likely don't know how to answer. I promise you that, when you've finished reading (and I've finished writing) *Trapped in My Mind*, you and I both will *probably* be better able to comprehend what is going on in any such situations we may be involved in or witness along the paths of our lives and will learn how to react.

We know so little about our minds and brains. I do know, however, that the mind has a limit. It can't take too much when it comes to handling the situations we deal with in a daily basis. There are multiple ways to cope in life. Some people drink to forget; others use drugs and other methods of altering themselves to defend or protect themselves. But sometimes, I would say more often than we know, the mind shuts down, perhaps because it's the only way the mind knows or chooses to manage a unique situation that could hurt us, whatever the situation may be.

I was inspired to write *Trapped in My Mind* for those who have come out from that state of mind, because they have fought, and they won. They were lost, and they found themselves. To all of you, my readers, my sincerest *congratulations*. You are strong and deserve the best of the best.

ABOUT ME

I was fifty-eight years old when my nightmare started. I am a female medical doctor, slim, and very outgoing. My life before getting remarried consisted of raising my kids—being mom, dad, and provider for about thirteen years. In those days, I felt strong, though I often felt weak at the same time. I was struggling a lot to make a living for my family. Literally, I was working 24-7, living more in hospitals than in my house. I needed to be strong to survive. I never complained. In life, you need to do whatever it takes to make it worth it. I was just living day by day in my precious island that was full of amazing memories with hidden secrets. Then everything changed.

During those years, I was waiting for a phone call from my ex-husband; I was waiting for these few words: "I want you back." It never came, meaning I am alone in this road, by myself as usual. I took it well, what else I can do, can't fight destiny.

I knew that my children were at that age when they needed me most. The days and weeks passed quickly, and time in general flew by. I did my best and gave most of me to my family and my career. I didn't realize that my inside was getting emptier. I was feeling like there was nothing left.

I remarried, this time marrying a man who traveled a lot due to his career. He was a project manager. We each had different careers with multiple responsibilities. I remember very well the promise that we made—that we would never live apart, no matter what. It was a promise that was never respected.

At present, I am actively working as a physician—or I was. I have been very grateful for my job, and I'm always very conscious of the responsibility of my career. I love what I do for a living. It's one of my passions. I have too much to give, too much to love. I used to enjoy the outdoors, dancing, swimming and feeling the waves and smelling the salt water, and everything that in some way fulfilled my days with energy.

Since I was a kid, I used to write here and there, just for myself. This time, I will share a deep experience that recently crossed my path and probably changed my life forever.

The situation I'm referring to occurred about a month prior to this writing, in May 2015.

Character One	Myself, strong, caring and very open-minded
Character Two	Myself, unable to point to anyone else, as too many people were involved, too many people were trapped with me in my delusions

CHAPTER 1

The Beginning

I was working out of state—to be more specific, Arizona. I was living in a nice hotel, the Residence Inn Marriott. The Arizonians were very open and talkative; I felt welcomed by them. I went to my training for this assignment, and it went well. I was excited to be starting a short-term job. It would last for about a month, so I would have new coworkers for a short period of time. By that time, my husband was again overseas, so I had chosen to travel. I didn't want to be alone anymore; there was too much of nothing and everything. So, I decided to travel

In Arizona, at the beginning, while driving my car, I started asking myself, *Is this the right move?* But I realized it was too late; I had already gone too far, and I would have to accomplish this assignment. In the beginning, I didn't know the roads. I guess that was normal, given this was my first time in Arizona. The first two to three weeks were not too different from my previous job. However, I will say that there were fewer hours of work. My patients had different illnesses. They needed to be taken good care of; they needed to talk and be listened to. I was excited because I knew that most diseases are not properly diagnosed, as people just hear but don't listen. My days went on with not too much change. I lacked sleep, as usual. I woke up every morning and started my routine— coffee, prayers, take a shower, get dressed, no breakfast (no time for that) jump in the rental car, and start my day.

Usually the days ran smoothly but were busy. I gave the best of myself with all the knowledge and love I could give. I never regretted the work, but again, there was not always time to have lunch. The day ended, and I got to the car and back to the hotel—to the loneliness, the empty room, with nothing and no one there.

However, as soon I was out of the work environment, strange feelings started filling my insides. I couldn't explain what was happening. Perhaps it was the loneliness, the lack of energy, feeling drained, and having no stamina at all. There was no life inside of me. I realized that I'd had these feelings for years, always masking them with a smile. The patients became family in my heart. *Hi, Sir/ Ma'am. How can I help you?* That was my introduction to each one of them.

In my personal life, I tried to give all of myself to my family. Those days were stressful; I needed to accomplish my mission in earth. I was living a life phase and wasn't paying too much attention to myself.

Looking back now, I realize that I had, indeed, been having those feelings and thoughts for years. I used to say, *Tomorrow will be better; everything will feel normal.* But what is normalcy? Nobody knows. Your body keeps moving forward, but your mind goes backward, stuck without any warnings. Did I ignore or deny some signs? Or did the necessity to keep working take my last drop of energy? These are questions that I still don't have the answer to and probably never will. You can run, but you can't escape.

CHAPTER 2

The Masks

I had lived alone for several years due to my husband's travels; my kids were growing, so I stayed behind. They grew up so quickly. My life then became bizarre; I didn't know where I belonged anymore. I had no expectations, no feelings. I needed love. Most of my life after that was spent in solitude in the woods in upstate New York.

Yes, we moved from my precious island to the states. I guess that's when my life started changing—started falling apart. In this new life, with new expectations, there were too many unknowns, too much of always hoping for the best.

I started a new practice, working long hours and long days. Again, I was always concerned that I didn't have enough time for my new family, much less myself.

Years passed with no change in my behavior. I changed masks every day. No one noticed my feelings; everybody was so busy demanding my presence.

My husband, on the other hand, traveled again and again. The eyes that I had fallen in love with were not as green now as I'd once thought them. We both had too much to hide; we were living different lives, and I no longer recognized this man. He was a stranger. I had no more memories; they were gone. There were no holding hands. I felt unloved, alone, and lost. I hadn't signed up for this.

I decided to change jobs, thinking that, perhaps, changes were always good. I was willing to create a new me with no more sorrows.

I started to travel, taking *locum tenens* positions—covering practices that were down doctors, covering doctors' vacations, or just filling in where extra help was needed. This was how I'd gotten to Arizona.

Another day ended, and I went back to my room. It would still be another four weeks before I'd made it to the end of this assignment. I continued with the same routine day after day—wake up, take a shower, get dressed, and jump in the car. Always I would be thinking, *Another day but a different challenge.* I was getting used to the surroundings already and no longer had to use the GPS to drive to work.

***

My husband decided to take a break and came to Arizona. We were together. We decided not to travel anymore and to start from scratch. We wanted to create new memories; we needed to start knowing each other again.

Our plans, however, didn't last. He stayed with me the first two weeks, and then he went back home. I felt disappointed, but again, I went with the flow. I was feeling like a loser. My instincts were telling me that something would go wrong.

I started feeling strange—different, lost, frightened, and abandoned. I wondered if perhaps this was the beginning of my death, the beginning of me slipping into a dark place.

***

Memorial Day weekend was coming soon. I was not excited, and I had no plans. I guessed it would be me and myself again. But something continued growing inside me; something strange was happening. Very gradually,

I started hearing voices in my head; they were very real, talking to and about me. Scary, eh? I thought I might be suffering from exhaustion and sleep deprivation. I knew that was not a good thing. Plus, I was not eating well, which also might be the cause of these hallucinations. Throughout my entire life, I had always found excuses for or answers to all my concerns and issues.

Was I in denial? One thing was sure. I always kept these thoughts just for me. I never shared them. They were probably growing deep inside me.

I do remember weird dreams—dreams that were extremely vivid and real. I didn't know if they were real or not. I was scared. Frightening, strange dreams and issues came into my mind.

I started feeling sick and knew that I had an infection. I had fever, chills, and gastrointestinal symptoms that I ignored. I had to keep working, and there was no time for me. I was feeling weak and dizzy. That's when I started thinking that I should reach out for help. So, in my confusion, I decided to go to the hospital.

The hotel called the ambulance, and the EMTS arrived and took me to the emergency room. The hospital was just walking distance from the hospital, but I did not know that. The staff asked me questions, which I don't remember well. They did tell me that I was dehydrated, and I was given fluids and electrolytes. I also remember that the doctor found me anxious and wanted to give me something for the anxiety. I refused the medication and had the urge to get out of the hospital.

When the hospital discharged me, the staff offered to call a taxi. But the hotel was so close that I decided to walk, even though I had no shoes with me. You might imagine how my walking was—I could see the hotel, but it took me about three hours to get there. I kept the hallucinations to myself and did not mention them, probably because, in my mind, they seemed real. Or maybe I was just exhausted. Oh God, I wanted badly to go home. But where was home?

I went to my room and decided to try to sleep or at least rest. But I couldn't. My brain was on fire; my body was numb. *Please, God, help me. Give me your strength. Have mercy.*

Then I decided to get up. Suddenly, I started seeing nets all over the room that seemed real in my mind. They had different shapes and were all over. I wanted to touch them and was surprised when I found I was doing it. In my mind, I knew that something was not right. So, I tried to continue my routine. It was a long weekend.

I was in terror that I was crossing the fine line between sanity and insanity.

And things started getting worse when I began to hear voices; I recognized the voices as belonging to people who were part of my normal world—people who I loved. Then the scariness was getting to me. I couldn't tell what was real and what was not. I was losing it. The voices didn't stop, and what I was seeing was getting worse.

The hallucinations become constant. Some of them were very painful; others I would call eccentric in a way that, at that very moment, I did not understand. And probably that was for the best. I started walking and wandering through the hotel, again with no shoes. But it did not matter. By that time, I was already trapped in my mind.

I did try to look normal to others, and I fooled myself—who can say I was behaving well?

I questioned myself: Did other people see and hear as well as me? That I will never know. I am pretty good at hiding my reality—at hiding myself and my sorrows and loneliness.

In a subconscious way, I was trying to look for help. I was texting and calling people who I trusted, just hoping one of them would sense the serious situation that I was getting into. I really wanted to see and touch someone real, not just hallucinations. The mind plays games, and I was already part of that.

I start hating the days and nights. I just wanted to sleep, but the voices of my brother and my sister-in-law were calling me I started walking all over the hotel and knocking on doors because the voices were coming from everywhere.

If just someone, anyone, had asked me how I felt or whether I was okay, perhaps—probably—I would have lied. I knew this was just the beginning of my mental derangement. But it did not happen.

Have you ever felt caring for the world in your back? Your silence tells me it's a yes. Have you ever feel that you can't give any more to anyone because you know that already you are gradually getting empty? I wanted to be the one on the other side—someone who received and felt cared for and loved.

The mind plays tricks in mysterious ways. There is so little that we know and understand about the mind, the brain. Mine was really playing with me. There was a moment that I did not know what was real or just my imagination. Or probably everything was the true reality. It was all so vivid that I could no longer handle it.

CHAPTER 3

The Trap

After that day, which was a Friday, everything started falling apart. From there, it went downhill fast. My mind couldn't stop. I knew there was no escape for me. I was scared to death, but there was nothing I could do about it. I fought back because I knew the outcome. But I was weak and frightened. During all that time, I'd no water, no food, and no sleep. I was *trapped* in my mind.

I started seeing my husband behind my bed. He would be trying to install FBI equipment with cameras that would allow him and everyone else who had the same equipment to hear and see me. I tried to talk to him, telling him to leave me alone. I would tell him that I knew what he was doing and that he was in the hotel. But he kept hiding and would disappear again and again.

The nets—in the shapes of animals and trees and other things—were driving me to cry out loud, "Stop, stop!"

The nets were getting worse. I started seeing them wherever I went. I would reach out to touch the animals, and in my mind, I did indeed touch them.

I decided I needed help, so I called the police. I dialed 9-1-1 from the hotel.

I was walking in the hallways and quietly telling people who I didn't know what was happening. I was probably begging for someone to pay attention, to really listen. I needed someone to help me. I called 9-1-1 again. Or was it the hotel that made the call? I don't recall. I was paranoid.

The police came to the hotel and searched my room, looking for alcohol, drugs, or who knows what. Nothing was found—not even the nets that were driving me literally insane. I did not explain to the police that my room was changing constantly.

CHAPTER 4

The Hotel Room

My hotel room was like a carrousel; it's difficult to explain. On the Friday night of the Memorial weekend, I saw a different scenario there. It resembled a competition to join a club or fraternity of some sort. I saw that on the second floor of my room, which I did not have.

There was this reunion of people who I had never met, except for two people whose names I will change, Mike and Jim. The people participating in the competition had to do certain things that were disgusting and beyond my comprehension.

This was a party for rich people, who were eccentric and, by my judgment, given what I was hearing and seeing, utterly lacking in morals. I don't remember well all that was going on because I was trying to hide. The others, mostly Mike, were trying to convince me to play. I refused, even if that meant I would have to pay consequences at the end. They were playing sexual games. I say that because they had to kiss someone and do other things that, out of respect for my readers and a desire not to be more explicit, I will leave out. Just take my word.

I tried to sleep because I didn't want to see whatever they were doing. Meanwhile, my room was changing depending on their game. I was mostly in the water. It was like a horror movie and grew painful with different phases in their game. I remember gunshots and people dying because they couldn't pass the next phase that they needed to accomplish to be part of the exclusive club

While all this was happening, there was always someone watching me, all the time. All I could do was try to run away from that nightmare.

Even if I tried to describe the world that was in my mind, I would not be able to do so. That memory was very painful, confused, and disturbed. You, my readers, will understand that. And for that I am thankful. There are likely other memories that are blocked as a defense. Each episode was created by the dark side. Therefore, I will not remember what hurts the most.

I guess that I slept on and off. I woke up just as the get-together was almost done. Mike was asking over and over how I was doing. Apparently, he was kind of ashamed and did not want to talk to me. The shooting was over.

I never figured out what was truly happening. I did hear that there would be a big get-together for those who had passed all the phases of competition and would now be members of the club or fraternity. I was utterly confused and mad about the situation.

The following day, I felt more disturbed and confused than ever. I didn't know what was real or what wasn't. I started praying. I still had one week more of my assignment. Would I be able to do it?

CHAPTER 5

The Hospital

Memorial Day came, and I knew that I would not be able to go back to work. I did, however, try to go. I walked to the car, but I fell and hit the back of my head. I crawled to the lobby, where I collapsed. Again, an ambulance arrived, along with the police, and I was taken back to the emergency room. The police officers and the EMTs convinced me to go to the hospital.

This was a very bad experience. I could hear them laughing, with a complete lack of compassion, joking about my hallucinations. I answered all their questions during the episode. I heard the words *crazy*, *alcohol*, and *drugs*. I wanted to scream, but I knew that, if I did, they would not let me leave the hospital.

I wanted to get out of the hospital, but I wasn't allowed

to leave. The hospital staff used the Baker Act, allowing them to involuntarily institutionalize and examine me for my own safety. Safety from what? I was already in danger. My cognitive functions were gone. What was right or wrong?

Finally, I convinced the doctor, telling him the truth. I would be flying back home in less than forty-eight hours. The hospital let me go. But why didn't they medicate me with something? My head was ready to explode. Did they have less cognition than me? It's just a matter of common sense. Here is a woman who is very anxious. And she is planning to fly alone? How about, let's protect her with something mild until she gets home? It didn't happen. Why didn't I ask? Perhaps I didn't want the hospital staff to think I was looking for pills. Prescribing medication was their job, not mine. I was a patient. I can't be my own doctor.

I did call my husband, my brother, and I don't know who else. Probably I texted or called a few people. I was weak and dizzy. I hadn't had any water or food for about four to five days. My husband told me to forget my assignment. He knew something major was happening in my mind and asked me to come home. I agreed and waited until the following Tuesday to call in sick.

CHAPTER 6

Survival

Those hours in between then and Tuesday were difficult. I spent the entire time looking for my brother and sister-in-law in the hotel—with no success. They were never there. I already had a flight booked in less than twenty-four hours. My question was, will I be able to drive? I wanted someone taking me to the airport, but no one was with me.

In the hotel, I started packing and praying for a safe drive to the airport. I was more concerned about hurting someone with a car than I was about my own safety.

That night was when I really felt that my brain was almost at an end. I knew that I had lost control of my brain. I gave up. I was seeing ghosts in my front yard in New York. I think that I called my husband. I was seeing them through the home security that we had in our house. I even took pictures of them. I know now that I was having visual hallucinations.

My flight was around 2:00 p.m., and for reasons that make no sense, I started driving very early in the morning. It was about 6.00 a.m. when I arrived to return the rental car. The drop-off location was in the opposite direction from the airport, and it was a chaotic moment. Picture a petite woman carrying heavy luggage and trying to get a shuttle for the airport, all while listening to voices and talking to herself and to people created in her mind.

Finally, I got to the airport, knowing that my mind was in outer space. Did my family realize that I needed company—that I was begging for help? I guess never told them. Again, I am pretty good at hiding my reality and feelings.

I realized that I was a woman reduced to a single instinct—survival until I made it home.

Okay, I had made it to the airport. I was still thinking, *why he dares to leave me alone?* I had likely come to the airport early because I wanted to escape. Remember, by that time, I'd already hit the bottom. What was happening to me? I called Mike, and he was surprised that I had arrived at the airport so early. I asked him where he was but never had a clear answer. In my mind, I understood that a friend had flown him back to New York. I remember telling him that I didn't believe him. But did I really call? I was still having doubts about who had been with me in Arizona. I had seen and talked to many people but never face-to-face.

Dragging my luggage through the airport was exhausting. I got to the airline check-in counter and was met with another disappointment. I was too early. I couldn't check in. It seemed I would have to wait about three to four hours before I could check in and be relieved of the luggage. Just remember, my readers, my mind was not right. I was still confused, cloudy, and foggy. I knew that I was on my own. I needed to hide my madness.

I called my family again. We probably spoke in a way that made me feel safe. I don't remember the conversations. But I was seeing the nets all over the airport. I think that I talked with some people about whether they were seeing what I was experiencing. Did they say yes? I don't recall. The entire time I was listening voices—voices belonging to Mike, Jim, and other members of the family. Jim was a friend of my husband's. Mike, who by my judgment was the one who'd invited me to participate in that strange "party," was real in the real world. I'd never gotten a very good sense from him. Perhaps that was why he was part of my insanity world.

I was listening everything the voices were saying. Mike asked Joe if he could send the chopper to pick me up. I wouldn't catch his answer. In my mind, it didn't matter. I was lost. I decide to make the best of my horrific situation. I placed the earbuds of my headphones in my ears and started listening to music and, occasionally, dancing. Can you picture that scenario, my dear friends? I now remember that I heard my nieces talking about me. They were saying, 'That's my auntie, always dancing and singing.' That was sweet. At least for me while I was dealing with my disturbed mind, hearing their voices was like seeing a rainbow on a cloudy day.

That day was probably the longest day of my life. I wandered through the airport, and all my senses were sharper than ever. I could hear what people were saying, or at least I thought I could. At the same time, my family was planning with the airlines and airports to be sure I would take the right plane. I knew I was confused but could not explain how. I knew in my mind that my brothers and my husband were watching me. They were telling me to get something to eat. Did I or didn't I? I was constantly looking up to try and find them. But they keep disappearing. What was happening?

When I passed security, looking for the gate was an effort. I do remember that I called my family again. Somehow, I knew they were helping me. Mike told me that a doctor had cleared me to get on the plane. I don't recall. My mind was blocked, trapped, and confused. I do remember talking with people while waiting to board the plane. I asked them if they were seeing what I was seeing. Some of them told me that, yes, they were, and those net games had to be prohibited in public places. I agreed and almost called them. I don't know if I did. Between the voices in my head and my surreal world and possibly imaginary people, I wasn't sure about anything.

Finally, people started boarding the plane. I was one of the first to get on the plane. An attendant brought a wheelchair. I was embarrassed, but I knew that my family had made those arrangements for me. I heard people in the room saying that I was taking advantage. Those comments made me feel awful. But deep inside, I wasn't me. I felt like I was possessed by an unrealistic world, perhaps created by the deepest memories of my lifetime. Or maybe what was going on in my mind was just a way to cope with life. It was like a life cycle, on and off. Perhaps it was a function of the brain, shutting down when you feel pain in your soul and know that there's nothing or no one that can help you, pulling you out of the big black hole that was growing fast?

I was already seated in the plane. Well I am lying. That person was seated, not me. That person, who was created by unknown circumstances, was experiencing the other side of normalcy, already crossing the line from sanity to insanity.

What I am going to write now was unbelievable, but it really was happening—I mean, in my thoughts, it was so real. The plane had a delay. I don't remember how long the delay lasted. Meanwhile, I started hearing voices. This time, some of them were not recognizable. But I knew others very well. They brought old memories from my childhood.

CHAPTER 7

Old Memories

For you, my readers, to understand the mysterious and vivid mental experience I had in the plane, I will share with you part of it. I was raised in a small town, walking distance to the shore. It was a very traditional place, in which we locals all knew each other. During holidays, we would all celebrate in the middle of the town on the holiday itself. During festivals, we would dress in accordance with the celebration. I remember very well that, during the holy week, we dressed to mimic the suffering and sacrifice of Jesus. We celebrated almost all the festivals and, as I said, always dressed according to the holiday at hand.

Now getting back to the plane, the voices were telling me about the glory of God. In my confusion, it was the

Holy Week that we were celebrating. I was hearing songs and Psalms that I recognized and knew. So, in my mind, I created a scenario, and those people close to me were the actors and actresses. I know it sounds very weird but in my mind, was quite real. We were taking videos and capturing pictures. All the time, I knew that something was wrong. Deep inside, I was frightened. The actors were changing costumes. We were creating them. Or was it just me? There was a theater, well kind of. I recognized voices of people from my town. They were in the same mind-set that I was in. Again, everything was being created and was so real. What was happening with my brain?

I enjoyed that part of my madness. We, or I, had a mission—to spread Christianity to others. I was sitting next to a gentleman in the center seat. From what I recall, he was telling me stories from the old days. I think he was just showing some kindness and compassion. Did he catch on that I was crazy?

This flight to Baltimore was long and complicated. I was very confused. I was lost again. This time, I was living a different life. I went back to the past, to my childhood.

I remember that some people were saying that we could be sued, as my entire crew was also taking pictures.

The problem was that we hadn't asked permission to do it. How much was real, I don't know. Everything, in my eyes, was true—vivid and clear. We decided, while still in the plane, to share the pictures and phone numbers to protect each other in case of a legal problem. And we would edit all pictures and videos to share with others, like in a theater. I don't remember if we did it.

CHAPTER 8

Watched

The departure time for my next flight was very close by the time we landed. Can someone, anyone help me? I ran to catch the plane. I needed to go home. The plane waited for some of us because of the delay that we'd had in Phoenix. Finally, I was on my way home.

However, I created another story. This time, I was seeing people looking at me and talking about drugs. I was very scared because I don't use drugs, much less carry them. I was paranoid. I saw police officers, who were always looking at me. And in my mysterious mind, the flight attendants were constantly trying to get in my bag to look for drugs. Along with the police, strange persons were always watching me. They were all over. While the plane was flying, I could see them on the roof of the plane. It was very odd, but that's what was happening in my reality. It was a nightmare. Or had it never happened?

It was a relief when the plane landed. However, I didn't know if the police would be waiting for me in Albany. My paranoia was getting worse.

I don't recall anything that happened in the airport. I just wanted to go home. I don't remember when I saw my husband. I do remember, though, that I told him something about drugs and that I was being watched. His face was calm, but something was wrong. I could feel it.

We got into the backseat of the car. My stepson was driving. Immediately, I saw a girl in the passenger seat. I asked him if she was his friend, but she kept disappearing. I started seeing nets again. I was furious because I thought that they were playing games with me. After that, I saw my husband talking on his cell phone. He was talking with my brother. They wanted to take me to the hospital. I was refusing and yelling at them. I was beyond tears. Finally, they convinced me to go to emergency room. I told them that I would go just for a few hours. It was nighttime.

I was exhausted inside and outside. I was mad at them. They were not taking me home. They were driving to the hospital. I didn't want to go. I wanted to see my house and my dog. But they didn't listen. I think that I talked with my brother, and he convinced me to go to emergency room. He calmed me down for few minutes. Meanwhile, I was in the car feeling frightened. A car was following us. What was it that they wanted from me?

In my delusions, everybody had a conspiracy against me. Why was this is happening? Why were they after me? I kept saying to my husband that he needed to get my backpack and my purse and hide everything from them. There was nothing to hide. I was, perhaps, hiding myself from reality, from the darkness of my nightmare.

CHAPTER 9

Let Me Go

I was confused and disturbed. The voices never stopped, and I was seeing people who were just in my mind. The emergency room was a nightmare for me. I saw all my brothers and nieces, my entire family. They were talking about me at the beginning in the hallways. I felt embarrassed and I think that I started hating the place. I was screaming at nothing. The hospital gave us a private room. I remember calling my daughter, but she was part of my imagination. I wanted to see my son, but everything was happening so fast that I could completely lose it.

I don't remember too much about the emergency room. I did hear over and over the same question: "Do you drink or use any type of drugs?"

My husband's response was always no, the same response that I gave. Everyone was concerned that it was likely that, in Arizona, someone had poured a hallucinogen substance in my glass or had somehow gotten me to eat psychedelic mushrooms. I understood their concern, but I couldn't see how that might have happened. "Please release me. Let me go."

I do remember the doctor was a female. She was very patient and sweet. After that, all the memories were blocked. My family would later tell me that I went into a catatonic state for about six hours. Just imagine the shock that they went through. Through the entire nightmare, they were dealing with a different person than the one they knew. Picture someone that you love in a fetal position, immobile, making only involuntary movements. Frightening, eh?

When I woke up, I didn't know what was happening. Set me free. I beg you.

I don't remember if I was still in the emergency room or in a different room that I had been transferred to. I was very confused. The visual and auditory hallucinations continued. I do remember that I was feeling more and more furious because I wanted to be in my house. I will summarize my behavior by saying I was *out of control.* I know now that my family and my husband were in contact during the entire time.

My husband told me that a good friend had come to the emergency room while I was in the catatonic state. He had prayed for me. I do remember having a holy rosary in my hands. I never asked how or when I had gotten it or who had given it to me.

I was waiting for my brother and sister-in-law. (Out of respect to them, I will change their names and call them Ed and Jen.) They were with me in Arizona, remember. I was looking for them. They were like my helpers. I remember that I called Ed and explained my mysterious and strange encounters with the nets. And I do remember that he had calmed me down. He was always with me through my mysterious illness, even when he was not there in real life. I wanted badly his presence to be there for me. But again, it was all delusions.

I remember the tears of my husband, but I was unable to comfort him. Everything was unbelievable and unpredictable. I was in my own world, probably taking a break from *life.* I realized that I had prayed a lot to have that break. It was happening, and deep inside, I wanted to escape from that nightmare or break from my life. I couldn't run. I couldn't escape.

Many people came to draw blood or to take me have many imaging tests. Not one time did one of them tell me what they were going to be doing with me. Or perhaps they did, and I don't remember. My brain was spinning and never shut down. I was confused, wasted, drained, and scared to death. How long I was out, I don't know. I probably refused to know. It was too scary.

My paranoia didn't stop but only got worse in the hospital. I couldn't trust anyone. I was seeing and hearing bad things, all about me. They were trapping me. I wanted to run away. I think that I tried to tell my family about my paranoid thoughts, but they didn't believe me. How much time had passed already? What was happening to me? I had to fight this, but how? I was sick, mentally ill. I knew that. It was time for me to start healing. Did I will have the strength? Doctors and nurses were always in and out of my room. My husband looked devastated. There was nothing I could do to help him.

Finally, Ed and Jen came. They were in Florida and took a plane to be there with me. I still remember their faces; they looked sad and scared. They tried to explain why I was in the hospital. They had to understand that

I wanted to go home. I had come from the airport to a hospital. I needed to understand that I was seriously sick. My situation was getting worse. Oh my *God*. Help me.

I needed to start trusting again. That had to be the first step. Otherwise, I would never be me, but rather, the woman who was now reduced to bones. My weight was in the seventy pounds. My mind was blocked to reality. I was trapped. I needed to start saying that I was no longer hearing voices or seeing things. Otherwise, I would be in the hospital forever.

I don't remember when my son came. But I do know that, because of that nightmare, I started fighting for my sanity. That moment marked the fight that only I alone could battle. For me, getting better was imperative. I didn't want my son; whose name is Fred to suffer. Fred meant a lot to me. He had flown from Jersey to be with me. Even though I knew I was withdrawn from real life, I had the will to come back from the underground that I had been in for who knew how long at that point.

Seeing my husband and my family made me stronger. This couldn't defeat me. This would not break me. Everything seemed unreal. I had to re-embrace reality.

I was admitted to the hospital for six long days, unable to sleep, and desperate to be discharged. I believed that the doctors didn't know how to handle my paranoid psychosis. My life had jumped from functional to completely insane.

Gradually, I started hearing fewer voices and seeing fewer imaginary people. I needed to go home. Please, I begged, give me the opportunity to be reborn in my own environment.

Finally, I was discharged, still feeling cloudy and foggy. My doctors told me that was normal, and gradually they expected the symptoms to lessen.

We went home. Fred took some time off to be with me. I was weak and dizzy; I was literally almost bedridden for six days. Gradually, I started doing simple things around the house. I think this helped me gain strength. I started eating, which was very important for my recovery. The family went back to their own routines. I was feeling more normal, though I was still foggy.

One day I took out my phone so that I could see the ghosts that I had been seeing while I was in Arizona. I also wanted to see the pictures and videos that I had taken in the plane. It was a scary moment—until that day, everything was very abstract; now I had evidence.

There were no pictures, no video, and no ghosts. All that I saw was darkness, and the videos just showed me talking with myself. I know now that I was *trapped in my mind*.

CHAPTER 10

The Unknown

My lessons from this mental breakdown remain unknown. Whether this might happen again is unpredictable according to my doctors. I am scared. I don't know how tomorrow will be and, even more frighteningly, what the next second might be. For now, I live day by day, knowing that we are very weak, and that *tomorrow is unknown*. And yet not knowing the outcome of this nightmare make me incredible vulnerable; but I do know that I will let you know and keep you posted as months passes.

I am a woman just coming out the other side of an acute psychotic episode. I was feeling confused, and now I feel concern about my future. There are too many uncertainties. Will this nightmare become a recurring episode in my life? It's a mystery. No person can give me a straight answer. I am trying to move forward. Most importantly, I need to convince myself that the episode will never reoccur. It's supposed that avoiding stress, confrontations, and problems will help prevent another event. Yeah right. Life is full of these very things.

That's why I decided to write *Trapped in my Mind*. I wanted to vent my emotions and feelings before they get away from me.

For you, my readers who, for whatever reason, have been in that mysterious world that I visited, believe in yourself. Use all your power and fight. Just remember that whatever doesn't break you makes you stronger. I will continue to keep in touch with you. Meanwhile, hang in there. This short book is written in a way that might be hard to understand, but I still feel cloudy. I've experienced no more hallucinations since leaving Arizona. However, after the episode that occurred there, my thought process has been hurt in some inexplicable way. Again, you will know about me in a near future, I know that the tomorrow it's unknown for you and me, we want to know what will be next, don't you?

As of this writing, a month has passed since I got home, and I must learn how to deal with and understand the aftermath. It will not be easy. That's a fact. However, I will learn again how to recover my mechanism of defense and to cope with the daily situations in life. I've been thinking about that mental episode. What generated and triggered it? It might have been a combination of factors that caused the carrousel inside my brain. What scares me is one simple question: What if happens again? I don't want to see those nets ever again. The visions were very disturbing, and I am afraid that it is likely that, next time, I will not come out.

Life is a cycle. Everything comes in episodes, back and forth. You don't know what might happen soon. No one does. Perhaps the answer to a pressing question you have is unknown, even for your doctors; they cannot give you a clear answer. I am living day by day, trying to make the best of each day. But honestly, it's difficult.

I have been going back in my life, trying to put the puzzle together, and I have realized that my mind never shut down. Ever since I was a child, I have always been speeding, night and day. Even my sleep deprivation has been abnormal in the last ten years. I knew it was not right, but I had no time to think about my health.

I guess that the healing process will be longer than I thought. I can't escape from my reality. I was sick. I was very ill, and the paranoia and the psychosis indeed happened. I am grateful that, in my crisis, I didn't hurt anyone (while driving). And I am also lucky that I was not hurt, physically at any rate.

I must think about every day like it's the first day of my life, not the last one. Perhaps I must make changes in my life to prevent stressful situations and learn again to regain peace inside of me. Nobody else can do it, just me. It will be a difficult path, but I don't have any other choices. I can't go backward; I will not have another mental breakdown. I am willing to learn more about how to live with myself and my surroundings, wherever that journey takes me.

I refuse to be trapped in my mind again. I am a survivor, and I must remember that I escaped from insanity and returned to the world, like it or not.

CHAPTER II

Before and After

I will give you some advice on how to keep your mind clear—how to avoid falling prey to a predisposition to lose your mind. I will share with you a part of my life that I think had some importance to my mental health. I used to live in a log cabin in the woods on a forty-three-acre property. It was a very quiet place. This was around 2005. By that time, my husband was traveling as usual. My brother Alf came to visit me in 2006, and I remember some words he spoke to me. We were on the porch, when he looked at me and made this comment while holding my gaze. "This place is beautiful," he told me. "But be careful. Too much solitude will get to you. It might trick your mind."

That was probably the beginning of my nightmare. Who knows? But indeed, he was right. It started with insomnia and the need to always remain vigilant—on the ready in case something was to happen against which I needed to protect myself. My neighbors were apart from my house. The neighbor across the street was an insecure and nosy woman with an evil heart, always trying to help me in some way. I tried to ignore them and to ask them to please respect the boundaries that were already in place. This was also a very disturbing time of my life.

This neighbor (I don't recall her name) was constantly trespassing onto my property. For what reason? I never knew and never cared. But I do remember many nights when I would find her there uninvited.

I tried to avoid her as much as I could, but she knew my daily routine. I lived about one hour from my place of work. During winter, it took me longer to get to the job, due to icy roads, deer, and plenty of snow. I was okay with that.

Meanwhile, my neighbor across the road was playing filthy games with me. I kept on my land expensive tiles and equipment. She used to put a sign up on my property that said, "Free," encouraging people to take my property.

That made me mad. The police told me to do whatever was necessary to protect myself and my property.

There were snowy nights that I spent hidden and waiting for her. Let me be clear. These concerns were very real; it was not paranoia. It was living a nightmare. I needed to get out of that mountain. I needed my freedom and my space.

I decided to move out from my piece of mountain. I couldn't take it anymore. I moved to an apartment, where I lived for about eleven months. That situation didn't last, as I was not used to living surrounded by noises.

Once again, I was looking for a place to live. I found a place close to my job but at the same time in the woods. I loved it, but again loneliness and solitude were my primary companions. At that time, I was dealing with breast cancer. For two years, I underwent surgery after surgery,

I managed well. Or I thought I did. I don't know now. After my episode of psychosis, I've started having doubts about everything. After living in that beautiful place for a couple of years, I moved again, this time out of state. I headed to Florida. The place I decided to give a chance this time was a beautiful home that my husband had bought for me. But I was alone with my dog. My neighbors were amazing, good people. One good friend, Col, was my savior. I was giving up on life. Now that I am looking back, I see that I did have a nervous breakdown because of many negative factors that were happening in my life in those days.

My husband seemed to not understand my situation or was in denial. After a year and a half, my neighbor called him, and told him that I was falling apart. I wasn't eating, I wasn't sleeping, and I had no life. Given this, he decided to come home. I was not doing well. At my job, I was doing well. I don't know how. But I push myself over the edge. I started falling apart inside and outside. Waking up in the morning was a challenge. I was, at that point, completely broken; pieces of me were strewn all over, some missing, some lost forever. That was the beginning of the end—the end of my sanity. I was too close to that fine line.

Please, I thought, *I need help. I want to stay on this side of the world.* I wanted to stay in the world where I could function—let me rephrase, in the world where I could use a mask to hide myself. Everything was chaos. I couldn't stand working with corporations that just cared about money, working long hours. I was living with a husband who was absent under the same roof. I tried many times to find him, but he was a stranger. I didn't recognize this new man. I didn't know what to do. Choices, choices—I was never good at that.

I was feeling the same with my husband home as I had without him. Our lives had drifted apart, big-time. What should I do? I didn't want to be hurt anymore. Should I walk away or not? I was at this point in my life where I didn't care. Many times, I felt the urge to run away and not look back. But we talked about starting from scratch again. Did I want that? I didn't know. There was too much uncertainty. I resigned from my job and again thought about moving. I was not sure about anything anymore. I was mentally exhausted. I had exceeded the limits. I would follow the flow.

Then we moved to North Carolina, another nightmare. He moved first. Meanwhile, I was living in our boat, which was different and interesting. The waves used to wake me up. I was different by that time. I was trying to enjoy life, whatever that means.

North Carolina didn't last either. My husband's work had promised that he would be home every night, but that was not the case. We then moved back to Florida and, in less than three months, to South Africa. That didn't last either, for many reasons that I will share with you one day, my readers.

As soon we returned to Florida, we discussed our situation and decided to go back home to New York. I drove to New York to look for a job and housing. It was not a pleasant journey. I was bouncing between interviews and looking for houses with my friend Lola, who was our realtor, but with no success. That road trip gave me a bad taste. My senses were telling me that something wasn't right, but I did drove back to Florida with several contracts on my hands. I chose the one I thought was best for me. We then moved to a rental house while my husband was looking to buy a house.

Finally, we found a place close to a lake in the woods. I chose that house. It turned out to be another chaotic situation, another bad choice. The place where I started working was impossible due intimidation and discrimination. But I did my best and have no regrets. My drive to work was about an hour in good weather. I resigned after sixteen months of what literally felt like hell.

Meanwhile, during those months, my husband was always looking for jobs, and he went to Panama. I was answering recruiters' offers. That's when I decided start taking *locum tenens* positions in different states.

The job in Panama didn't work out, so I knew that I had to work. I had already compromised myself by agreeing to work out of state. After all, the odyssey that would ensue, as you already know, would affect me forever.

The lesson that I have to share with others is this: We need stability. We need a peaceful environment. And most important, we need to avoid too much solitude. Alf, you were right. The loneliness and the instability got on me. Please live in stable situations, with peace in your heart and mind. Eat healthfully, sleep well, and don't hesitate to ask for help. Don't feel ashamed. It is what it is. Have good friends and be thankful every day for what you have and don't have. Trust me, there is a reason.

CHAPTER 12

Rebirth

The change I now must make in my life will be a long and probably hard process, but my faith will give me the strength and the resources for a complete healing. It's like a rebirth. What's meant to be will be. I am now taking baby steps, healing inside and outside. It will not be an easy journey, but it will be much better than the one I was on before.

As I was writing, I grew more concerned. Apparently going back over my life made me acknowledge that I'd had a mild episode of nervous breakdown while living in Florida. It wasn't as bad as this recent event, but the fact that it did occur might mean that I am predisposed to these types of episodes. What happened to my mind in Arizona could recur at any moment and probably be worse. I must tell my psychiatrist about this previous episode. It's very important, as it will likely change the prognosis.

The strong woman that I thought I was disappeared. She doesn't exist. She was deleted by some higher power. I am just a very susceptible person with an uncertain future that vanished, frightening me. But no matter what happens, I will be calm and think positively. My future will be a long, unpredictable road. It won't be easy to stay calm and positive, but it'll be worth it—perhaps making the difference between me staying on the sane side or crossing forever the fine line between sanity and insanity. I don't want to stay in the cloud and this confusing world. I will keep fighting. Anyhow, in the end, what will be will be.

My tomorrow is in my hands. I must work hard from me, myself, and I. Everything and nothing matters anymore. Happiness, tranquility, and peace are upon me. Will I be able to handle the uncertainty, the unknown? There are no answers. I must simply live day by day.

I want to thank my husband, my son, my brothers, my sister-in-law, and my friends who were on my side while I was battling my insanity. I love you all.

My husband and family were really worried about me. I knew that, in the end, I couldn't describe how insane I was. I do know that everything in my mind was real, even though perhaps in the real world it wasn't. Or maybe it was, indeed, happening. I will never know. And neither will you.

DECISIONS: POEMS WRITTEN
BY THE AUTHOR

To trust or let it go, to live or just exist.
No questions, no answers;
Stay alive or choose to quit.
The brain chooses not to answer.

Choices, choices, challenges, challenges—
Did I have it right or not?
Decide to exceed my power to be happy,
Decide to fight for freedom and to linger in my mind.

Smell the roses, kiss the soil,
Ride a horse and enjoy the ride.
No more whys. No more questions.
Just kiss yourself and love yourself.

Stay still and stare at stars;
Stay still and make a wish.

No more questions waiting for answers,
Just there waiting for grace and greats.

Nothing happens for a reason;
Everything happens for a reason.
Just look up and beyond,
Faith and everything will go around.

Around what? Never mind.
All that counts is the rain,
The sky, the fall, the laugh, and being kind.
Keep it quiet and never mind.

Life needs inspiration, and what you do with that can change
How you go about living,
Fueling a life that will motivate you to get the most out of your lifetime
Be creative, be passionate, be you.

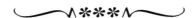

Broke never. Fight until your last breath.
At the end, what will be will be.
Good or bad, you won.
Swim. Feel the waves, and life will turn out how it will turn out.

Be grateful or not? That's a choice.
Be you, not what people want you to be.
No tears or tears? To laugh or not to laugh?
Inspire yourself for just you, and that will create a
New you, a better you, smarter and wiser. That's the clue
of living,
With and without tearing up
With and without laughing.

Too tired to carry heavy luggage.
Wind, take away from me what I don't need—
Everything that doesn't let me move on.
I just want to carry what fits in my pocket and my heart.

There must be a way, but which way?
To feel release, but how?
Feeling heavy, tight.
Wind, protect my mind.

Promises, lies, nothing matters. What will be will be.
Moving forward or backward, it's the same.
Choices, hope, nothing matters.
To stop or to continue, nothing matters. The unknown
Will be the same, because, at the end, what will be will be.

Being able to breathe is a gift
Being able to love
Feeling the air in your lungs
And not grasping for her, it's a gift.

Having thoughts without having them
Feeling empty knowing the answers.
Making love in your mind, no one with you
Smiling to nothing and crying for everything.

Be able to absorb the reality surrounding you
Without having it.
Life changes so fast that it's impossible
To keep up with the flow;
Carrying a heavy piece of luggage, when you
Know it's empty; having the feeling of drowning
In the deepest place, unknown.

Everything must go or
Everything must stay.
You know the answer.
Then go like a feather

Smooth, quiet
Fly, rest, don't look back
Don't look forward
Don't look at all.
In the end, it's everything or nothing.

There is something magic about fall
The red, yellow, and orange leaves—
Trees shouting out loud the Glory of God
Nature giving its beauty with no expectations.

Life is full of beauty and sorrows.
No time for complaint, no one to listen.
Life is full of things and emptiness.
No time to complain, everybody listens.

Yesterday, I had a dream, a dream of love
The love that never existed.
Yesterday I had a dream. You were in my dreams,
So far and so close that I tried many times to touch you

Did I? It was a sweet sensation so real that I did not
want to
Wake up.

L.P. MD.,

We were just together, staring at each other,
Talking about the future, the past, the present.

We did have a very complicated past, but one that was
full of love

We do not have a today. It was just a dream.
We talk about our tomorrow, the uncertain future.
When you walked into my life many years ago,
I was a young girl with expectations of happiness.
I want to continue pursuing happiness, us, but you've
drift so far from me
Even our future will be complicated. Or not?

Half of my life has been dreaming about.
What if? But again, the reality is now; you are not here.
You are not there.
I don't want to face it anymore.
I don't want to love you anymore.

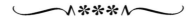

The fall always bring memories
Memories that are bred into my blood
Memories that are yellow, orange, and red
Like the fall in my place.

What if? Did I or we ever get an answer
Unknown.
What if? If I say yes, will it change something
Or nothing?

We all know destiny. Can she answer me back?
Do we still have a chance or not?
When the time passes, it never comes back.
Do we still have a chance or not …?

Yesterday, I had a dream.
Today, I remember the dream.
Tomorrow, no one knows.
Can I live in my dream?

Eternal moments, sweet and passionate
Days staring at the window, waiting and waiting
I know in my heart that someone above controls
Everything. My Lord, do I have the right to keep waiting?

Now neither reality nor you in my day;
Now the guilt, the tears.
My day today is like every other day
With you but without you, with love but not love.

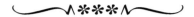

Ghosts that follow me, wherever I go
Reality that got lost
Ghosts from my past, my present
A future that doesn't exist.

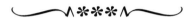

Difficult times in life—then fly, like an eagle
As high as you can, fast and far.
That way, you don't have to hide,
Just get away from the stormy days.

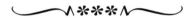

Just when you feel you are alone,
Breath, smile, touch.
Nothing to fear.
Run and follow the ride.

Secrets, just for me.
Don't want to sell my freedom.
Lies, never for me.
Don't want to live. That hurts.

Forgive—a decision that only you can make
Forget—never keep the hurt tucked in your heart
Trust—hard to put in pieces
What is broken can't be unbroken.

Too much luggage? Let it go.
Too heavy, I am drowning,
Need to throw things. Forgive.
Need to do it, let it go.

Forgiveness, it's a decision, not a feeling,
It's a choice that you make
Because that hate that you carry in your
Heart is heavier than you think

Unable to move on, unable to stay either
Decisions, decisions;
Can't reach the mountain
Can't swim the lake, much less the ocean.

Just let it go.
Something better will come.
Just let it go.
Something profound will come.

Life tests you—too many tricks, too much of everything
Too many deceptions, tears, choices.
Passing through life with fear of every second
With fear of knowing the unknown,
Passing through life with emotions of every second
Expecting from each minute, just You.

Big challenges that you need to accomplish
Deep and shallow. Doesn't matter; they are all the same
Daily challenges waiting for answers
Waiting for the unpredictable to happen.

Very simply, nothing is the same. We rotate like the earth
Depends on the moon and the sun; the gravitation
Takes you deeper in your thoughts, so deep
That you can't find yourself.

Do I want to see my real me?
Do I want to face myself?
No, it's too dark or too brilliant.
No, let me be without knowing.
Just let me be.

Holding thoughts that hurt
Holding thoughts that smile at the past

Passing through with deception and tears
Tears that no one sees, just You.

How much energy do I still have?
How much of everything?
And in the deepest part of my brain,
Just waiting for what?

Too many years waiting, too many years
Rivers of tears
Rivers of tears
Too many years waiting, too many years.

Yesterday, I had a dream we finally were together—
Too disturbing, not real.
Yesterday, I finally had you.
Too complicated, not real

Lighting a candle, waiting to see reality
Waiting for answers
Waiting with tears.
Lighting a candle waiting to see you, to see us.

L.P. MD.,

Taking chances, like rolling dice.
Not taking any.
Everything is a myth.
I will roll the dice again, waiting for luck.
No luck. Just reality.

Hard to understand the present
Difficult to forget the past
Much more unpredictable, the future.
What is hardest to predict, I don't want to know.

No expectations will be easier
Than no deception.
No expectations will be harder
Than no hope, no light, no peace.

What will be the best way to live in this
Unpredictable lifetime?
Just sit, smell the rain.
Thanks for everything.
Thanks for nothing.

Everything is easy to say but hard to follow,
Pursuing happiness, love, peace.

Earth, do you remember that I live here?
Do you remember my dreams and goals?

No, you don't. You go so fast, it's hard to catch up.
But yes, you know; I know you do.
Perhaps everything is in my head.
Perhaps this is the way it's meant to be.

More questions, more concerns.
Leave me alone, please.
Shut down, my brain. Don't want to think. Don't want
to expect.
Perceptions and dreams, are they the same?
They overlap in my head and heart,
Like a big wave, with a strong current
That breaks against the shore but doesn't stay.

The current is taking me to the deepest places, the parts
between the waves.
I can't see anything, can't breathe.
I need to get out of this rip.
Can't breathe. Please help.

Not easy to live, not easy to die.
A puzzle that you never finish.
A puzzle with missing pieces.
Not easy to live, not easy to die.

The cliff is too high and profound.
The thoughts are too intense and deep.
No. Nothing and everything.
Just me, my thoughts, and the pain.

Pain all over inside and outside,
Waiting for the reality to surface.
Hurt all over, broken heart
Unable to save, unable to rise.

Give me peace, give me serenity
Take away my sorrows.
Give me love and embrace me.
Take away my ignorance.

Yes, ignorance of the truth but what is the truth?
Ignorance of living.

Give me wisdom to understand the
Understandable and the strength to
Keep going between the dark and the light.

The dark is not that black.
The light is not that bright.
Whatever it is, I
Want to see, want to know.

I did have a strange dream: You, me, and my past.
I tried to make it true; it didn't happen.
I want this so badly, so seriously that, if I can change
In my lifetime or at least cut pieces of some probably—
and I say
Probably—the dream will come true.

I am kidding myself again. Mind, stop wandering.
Mind, stop dreaming.
Nothing was real, never was.
Just me and my voice, begging for a change

A change that will never happen.
I feel ill in my heart.
I feel strange, unique in my
Thoughts and feelings. Are they real?

L.P. MD.,

I want to go to another planet—I don't belong here—
Want to be invisible so no one sees me.
Please give my privacy back.
Don't look for me; don't waste your time.

I don't want to be found
Don't want to be hurt.
Give back my wings
Give back my peace.

Decisions, choices—overall, that's life.
I didn't have choices but indeed took
Decisions that I regret or not, not sure.
Both together make me who I am now,
A free spirit that can't find the way home.

On my way home. Where is home?
It's all over. Want to belong to something.
No way in, no way out,
Just deeper and deeper.

Not expecting answers or solutions.
Just here taking my inside to the outside.
Just here in my solitude
Waiting for a light showing me the road back.

Can't win; it's too strong. Can't win; it's too intense.
Trapped in my own decisions, no other choices.
I want to win though, want to be me again
Want to go home. Do you hear me? Want to go home
Where ever that is.

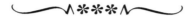

Don't whisper to me. Can't hear.
Talk loud, and I will follow.
Can't see. Be my eyes.
Don't want to miss the road again.

My love, can't find you. Are you lost like me?
My life, can't see it. Are you blind like me?
Need answers, need to recover my brain
Need to reinstall my life at day one.

If there is just a possibility of doing that,
I will take it.
Can't do it anymore; feel weak.
I surrender. Please forgive me and guide me.

No energy, feel drained, wasted, worthless.
Knowing the unknown
Will be the first part of my cure,
Will be the first step, the first sign of strength.

Waiting for that moment feels forever
Feels sometimes impossible
Waiting for that moment…
Then I will take the wheel and start before the beginning
Before the ending.

Fire in my brain, need water.
Fire in my soul, need peace.
Don't see answers, can't hear them.
Don't see the beginning until the end.

Want to fight negativism. Hard to do it.
Want to fly like a bird and disappear.
No need to be sad. It's my decision.
No need to look for me. Don't want to be found.

Living in a place that is not my place,
Living and dying at once.
No need for answers. Was a choice.
No need for nothing. Just write.

Giving myself to pages that can't be erased.
Giving everything that I am to you.
Receiving back more questions,
Receiving back memories that want to be erased.

No, please, don't erase the only thing that is left—
My memoirs.
No, please, don't erase them so I can learn
From them. Not sure what I want. Please, pain, go away.

Can't think properly. It's a roundabout
That keeps taking me to the same place
Over and over. No escape, no exit seen.
Trapped in my own thoughts, in my own life.

Did you ever feel the same? Or is it just me?
Did you ever feel lost, no way to go?
I did, and I am. Can't find the way to go back.
Can't find the road, can't find the road.

Hopeless and loneliness are two factors
Facts that stopped me from moving on
Facts that don't allow peace inside. I become part
Of my own destiny without asking me.

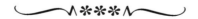

Deception and disappointment
Faith and hope
Pairs that walk together
Both with me all the time.

L.P. MD.,

Too many clouds, darkness
Too much hope, brightness
Which one will come first? That will be the answer.

No need to be with people to figure some things out,
No need to be alone,
No need to be in solitude or sadness.
Just need light, guidance to find my way to home.

Home is my past. Home is where my heart used to be.
Home is family. But where are they?
Oh, my Lord, give me your wisdom. Let me fight.
I am blind, but I can see people in the way they really
are, not in the way
They want us to see them.

I am here. Please don't forget me.
It's like dying.
I am here. Don't abandon me
I keep trying.

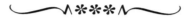

It's a cycle. No matter what I see or where I go
It's the same.
It's a vicious cycle, and the big ball
Brings you to the same place. No way to go.

I had a dream, a dream about you. Yes, you know who.
We finally met after almost forty years.
Do you remember? I don't. I keep losing my mind over
and over.
It was a long time ago, too many lost years.

Are you with me? Or I am with you?
Don't know. There is no us.
Silence and solitude
Silence within us, within our blood.

Big ocean of tears, detachment from reality.
No caring, no passion
No point of return
No point in what's going on around you.

I fly alone. I climb alone.
Having strong wings
Makes me go higher and higher.
Because I fly alone, I have the strongest wings.

L.P. MD.,

The power of love is greater than anything else.
The love of power is strong but selfish.
Write in your heart everything that matters.
Keep in your mind everything that counts.

It's not possible to give love with an empty heart;
It's possible to give love if you have it.
Today feels numb, without feelings.
Just fly in the cyclone and follow the winds.

Are you with me or not,
Life, are you?
Are you with me or not,
Death, are you?

Give your power to others.
Give me your power to finish.
Don't do it. I will be selfish
You do it. I will be grateful

Grateful for knowing that I am not alone.
Grateful for what?
No one is here, no one,
Only the dark space, no light for me, for us?

The church can tell some stories that I kept hidden.
No need to ask me. Just go and listen
In places, that if they can talk,
Will tell you my sins, my real inside.

I lost track of time, and all my dreams flew far away
Before they all came true.
Pursue them. Don't lose them.
They will never come back. They flew fast, and I am lost.

I must allow the strength of love to be reborn in me.
I need the tools. I need the instructions.
I want to change the world or simply
Want to change my thoughts. I need to change this
new me.

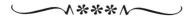

Everything is random—happiness, sadness, joy, madness.
Nothing gets resolved though.
Getting close to reality, scary. Don't know what to expect
I want everything gone. I want everything back. Very
bizarre.

But that's my life; my insight never shuts down.
Never give up, even though I do to get some relief from
my brain.
No questions. Ask neither question.
Just let me take a deep breath and fight with the infight.

Too much to think, too much hurt.
Need a break to restart my me.
Need a break to breath and feel.
Too much to forget—not in me, though.

If I can just reset myself, if that will help—
Who knows, again the unknown—
If I can just undo what was done,
Perhaps I might live in my life.

At present, I am not living. I am just here.
Can't take any more.
Choose to have a death while living
Choose to survive. Decisions, decisions.

Trust? That's a no. Neither forgive.
Being here without my presence
I am obsolete, don't count

Being just with my shadow that doesn't recognize anymore.

Mind
Sleeping, thoughts
Confused, mouth
Shut.

Whichever world I am in needs to release myself from me.

Awkward moment in my life. Don't know how to go back.

Go back where?
Go back for what? No matter
What, life is
Shut.

I can see me at the bottom of the sea, staring at the darkness of the moment, enjoying the loneliness inside of my solitude. I don't remember the brightest parts of life. Perhaps there is no life anymore. Or better yet

Probably the ocean is all I have now, showing me the Glory of Nature, so I can wake up from this nightmare that is swallowing my soul, my feelings, my dreams.

However, I want to get out. I want to know me again. I want to start a new life with the old me. This new me is trapped, and I used to be a free spirit. Now I am just these: a couple of words encrypted onto a piece of paper with no beginning and no end.

I see clouds through the clarity of the water, thirty feet under and thirty feet above. Unable to perform, unable to think straight, I am trapped by the dark inside my mind. Can I clear it? Can you clear it for me? Or is this just another weird thought? I can't remember. Help me remember, please. My entire life went upside down, and I am lost.

I am going to fight it, alone as always but with company at the same time—me and myself. I trust my cognition. I trust my mind even though it doesn't belong to me anymore. I am a stranger inside of myself. Oh well. Faith, keep me going—faith in the highest, faith in my instincts. Just Faith.

Today I wake up with something, with memories of when all this started, with memories that frighten me. I don't want to. Don't let me go again. Rescue is on its way. For whom? For me? For you? Again, unknown. Too much mystery, too much uncertainty. Just let me be; let me go.

No need for pity. I need to fight it. Therefore, stay with me and follow my path, follow my madness. You will see at the end the outcome, the unpredictability, me losing my mind and finding it again. You'll see the fine line between the unreal and the present chaos.

Everything is falling apart. Or is just destiny? Be with me all the way. Don't abandon me. Don't give up on me. I need your strength, your peace. I need to cross back over that fine line that is keeping me stuck, trapped. I don't want to be alone on this horrific road that started too long ago, and I can't stop.

Feelings—love, hate, scary things—don't want to be alone

Thought about you. Why? Don't know. Probably, I don't want to stay trapped, don't want to be stuck.

Life without living. Dying without death. Love with no love. That's all this is about. Questions with no answers. You all, at least respond once; be with me. I want to run and never stop, running and running just to get to that place where one returns from the unreturned. It's not easy; there are no guarantees, just hope, just hope.

Being myself without being me—sound sad? Incredible? But fighting is the only choice that I can see in my today, my tomorrow. Karma? No, everything is in my head, or nothing is in there. I don't know, don't care, for what? My present is empty. I've no memoirs, nothing to grab, nothing to remember.

To find my last chapter, I need to reopen everything, need to figure out how everything started and perhaps how everything will end. For what? And why?

I need to know. It might be the only way that I can close this chapter and move into the reality—just to be in it, just to be me again, without nightmares and madness in my mind.

REALITY VS UNREALITY

Tomorrow do not exist, just today
Yesterday it's over, just today

Always asking why me?
No answers , just silence
Can you help me find the truth of life? or I just
Have to remember that this is the way will be.

Come back to me and ease my path, come back to me
and make me real again.
The solitude is stealing my cognition, my future my
dreams.
My me, don't let me disappear, want to be here.

Don't dissapear , don't ran away from me. Too many
uncertainty too many unknowns.
The loneliness inside on me is burying me in the darkest
place in my neurons.

No turning back by myself, no nothing . Perhaps no matter what happens I need to continue fighting this fire in my brain.

Being this me really hurts, yet not being at all is something that is taking slowly my last
Breath, need air , need life , I am in need of everything, but everything might be
Nothing . Just love me don't abandon me don't forget about me . I am here , I am here.

Life is harsh, or we make it that way? I need oxygen to keep going
I need certainty that I am alive. The numbness and the ghost that live in me
Is killing my mind and yet I keep going , going where? Going nowhere.
Love life without life loving me or is the contrary? No matter what, even that I forgot the road.

The road of reality, my road, your road . Can they cross once , perhaps we will know , we will feel it.
Oh my oh my. I am blind; need to open my eyes so we both can see the same, we can then feel the same feeling without knowing it. It's strange and mysterious our reality, our relationship,

Do we have one? Or I just want to make one, don't know, don't remember, don't care , this is it.

I am here I am , waiting for my mind to come back , for the release of my trapped mind , waiting for
My senses to wrap the reality and bring the normalcy in an abnormal mind. Lost and found , lost and found that's how I am now, therefore can you believe me now? Can you understand me now?

My brain is screaming, on tears can't put the puzzle together, so dark , thoughts very intense that for now are not taking me anywhere. No senses or feelings, just emptiness.

Need the brightness of a clean spirit, need the love of my life holding my hands
Just be there or here for me but just be...

Live or die , options that will and might change the spectrum of everything.
Living in fear, living without laughs , without living
Can't be , I am for now retired from life , no benefits just dying living without knowing the way to go, the way to survive my vacations from the nightmare of my trapping.

Printed in the United States
By Bookmasters